CW01018042

Dance Not for Time

K . P . YOHANNAN

DANCE NOT
for
TIME

POEMS

BOOKS

a division of Gospel for Asia

www.gfa.org

Dance Not for Time
© 2013 by K.P. Yohannan
All rights reserved.

All Scripture quotations, unless otherwise indicated, are
taken from the King James Version. Public Domain.

Scripture quotations marked NKJV are taken from the
New King James Version. Copyright © 1982 by Thomas
Nelson, Inc. Used by permission. All rights reserved.

Illustrations by Sudyainis Hernandez and Jainis Hernandez
Cover design by Cynthia Young

Library of Congress Control Number: 2013951840
ISBN: 978-1-59589-129-7

Published by gfa books, a division of Gospel for Asia
1800 Golden Trail Court, Carrollton, TX 75010 USA
phone: (972) 300-7777
fax: (972) 300-7778

Printed in the United States of America

For information about other materials, visit our website:
www.gfa.org.

Table of Contents

Introduction

I don't pretend to be a poet. The truth is, I don't know all of the rules for writing poems, and honestly, I never expected to write poetry.

Many of these pieces came to me as I reflected on God's goodness or on little things that make me happy. Some came as I sat alone after conversations with needy and hurting souls or during the sad and helpless silence that came after encountering suffering Dalits and people living on the streets. Others resulted from reflections on the past, on stories and specific events that impacted my life in both big and small ways. Believe it or not, a great number of these poems were written on scraps of toilet paper, for it was there that I got the inspiration to write!

I am just a normal human being. I have struggles just like you and everyone else, as I think you will see when you start to read this collection. I am thankful for God's grace and mercy. I am also grateful for the affirmation of so many who are on this pilgrimage too, journeying toward another world while still living on this side of the door.

Thank you for your interest in reading. I hope these poems will strengthen and encourage you and somehow make your own story a little more meaningful and rich.

For the joy to come,
K.P. Yohannan

IT IS
GOOD

Creation

God
Eternity past
Time when there was no time
Stood on nothing
For there was nothing to stand on.

He spoke words
Words that only He knew what it meant.
"Let there be."

Out of nothing
With nothing
All things came into being.

Sun
Moon
Oceans filled with fish
Trees and forests of birds, bees, insects.

All creatures.
All.

And God said,
"It is good."

God.
Time began.
Everything existed.

His heart longed
For someone
To love.

He thought.
Talked to Himself:
"That's it. Let's do it."

continues

Stood on dust
Bent down
Handful of mud
With loving hands
As a potter with his clay
Gently molded
A copy of Himself.
With mud.

Man.

Blew into his nose
Breath of life
Mud became man.
Man with soul
Free to love
To choose.

"Just like Me,"
God said.

No one said a word.
So, He said it again:
"It is good."

Question:
"You searched all over to find a friend.
Did you find one?"

"No, God."

"All right.
Come near.
Don't be afraid."

Anesthesia
Feel so very tired
"Close your eyes for just a moment."
Heavy, deep sleep.

Surgery
One rib
Took it in His hand
Spoke the word.

Waking.
Wonder of wonders
Standing before him
Woman
Most beautiful
No comparison.

continues

Adam and Eve.

"Now you are
Husband and wife.
Love him.
Love her.
Love forever."

Hand in hand
They walked away.
God stood still
Watched
Smiled and said:

"It is good."

Walk with Me

Please
Come
Walk with me.

Take my hand
Feel my love
Touch my thoughts.

Talk to me
Dare with me
Don't fear
Love is real.

Narrow path
You close to me
Now as one
Come
Walk with me.

Morning Prayer

Good morning, Father
    You are my God.
I love You
    I thank You
    I am Yours.
Another day
    what a gift
Thank You!
Tell me
    Your plan for today
    I want to be a part of it
    It is going to be great.
Again I want to say
    thank You!
In Jesus' name
    Amen.

When Love Is Real

Two little pebbles
were cast
into the lake

Two little ripples
were made
in the lake

Those two ripples
became one
in the lake

So is friendship
when love is real.

Love Is . . .

Listening with the heart
Expressing your feelings
Sharing your heart
Telling your fears
Crying without shame

Remembering special days
Not forgetting birthdays
Writing a letter
Buying a gift
Writing a poem
Calling on the phone

Spending time together
Praying together
Going on a walk
Giving a hug
Holding hands
A loving look
Going places

Wearing clothes he likes
Cooking tasty food
Bringing coffee in bed
Waiting for him to eat

continues

Not holding back
Receiving with humility

Being there when children are born
Helping with chores
Buying her clothes

Not criticizing in public
Giving her room to grow
Not dominating
Responding, not reacting
Correcting when needed
Admitting when you are wrong
Keeping promises
Not comparing her with others.

A Blessing

Blessed by that day
The day you were born
    to share
        laughter
    to say
        a kind word
    to care
        for someone in need
    to know
        God's grace

Peace to you
My precious friend

Happy birthday.

Love Is Saying . . .

I think of you
I will call you
I will wait for you
I miss you much
I wish you were here
I can't wait to see you
Please come soon

I trust you
Only you
You are mine
I am yours
I can't think of life without you
Thinking of you
I need you

There is no one like you
You are my best friend
You help me live again
Called just to hear your voice
Nothing I want, just you
This waiting is killing me

I was wrong too
Please don't cry
It is my fault
Sorry
Forgive me
It is okay
I understand

I wrote to you
I prayed for you

No
Yes

Let me help
I'll do this for you

You are special
So glad you are you
I need you
I love you too.

Little Things I Like . . .

Tea in a clean glass
An old watch that runs
Tiny roadside tea shop
Thoughts that make me happy

Telephone that works
Fountain pen
Blue-black ink
Books with short stories

Winding roads with trees on both sides
Tiny birds that sing in the morning
A candle when the lights go out
A sincere smile

People who tell me when I am wrong
Preacher who doesn't scream and shout
Real flowers
A story that has a good end

Friendship not for benefit
A word of thanks
Friendly old people
Village children

Driving alone
Late-night omelet at a street shop
The thought of seeing you again
Clothes that feel comfortable next to my skin

Words of forgiveness
Intelligent people who are simple
Simplicity that is authentic
Hearing, "I love you too"

Questions that make me think
Answers that I don't have to give
Listening more than talking
Asking myself, "What if I were in their shoes?"

Leaves that dance in the breeze
Tears of joy
Touch of love
Listening to you
Sound of silence
Sunset in summer
Sitting alone in bed
     when I pray for you

What Can You Do?

"Little puppy, what do you want?"
The big horse snorted in contempt.
"You are wasting your time in this house;
The Master has no use for dogs like you.
I carry the loads and pull his cart—
And you, a tiny thing—what can you do?"

The little dog was hurting inside;
He walked away with a heavy heart.

A cow mocked, too, with words as sharp as a sword:
"The milk I give makes me, you know,
The most valuable thing on this farm.
Dogs like you are a pest
We don't ever want to see you again!"

The rest of the animals joined the cow,
Each one boasting of his or her use.
Chickens prided themselves in the eggs they gave;
Cats boasted in the mice they caught.

Now the puppy was truly sad
And began to sob out loud.

An old dog had been listening to all of these claims;
He called the puppy to his side.

"They are right," he said to the little one
"You are too tiny, and you know it well.
But you must do what God made you for—
And that is the thing that matters the most."

That evening the Master came home,
Tired, exhausted and weary from work.
The puppy ran and jumped into his arms,
Loving his Master with all of his heart.
Joy sprang into the tired man's heart,
And he fell on the grass with the puppy in his arms;
Hugging and petting, he spoke these words:

"You make me happy, my little one,
You are my best friend, and I love you so much.
Even if I had to give up all else
I would never leave you, my little friend."

The rest of the animals heard these words;
They hung their heads in silence and shame.

Nothing is more important
Than love, my friend.
Love others,
And you will never be alone.

WHERE

ARE

YOU?

Paradise Lost

Paradise was lost long before our time, yet I cannot help but be fascinated with it. Sometimes I play the events over in my mind. This poem is part of that movie in my head.

Paradise:
>> beauty unimaginable.
Flowers
>> all colors
>> all combinations
>> deep green leaves
>>> dancing in the breezes
>> dew drops sleeping
>>> in the cradle of roses
>>> rocked by breezes
>>> to the mockingbird's song.

Rivers ran clean
>> swarming with fish
>>> of all kinds.

Tall, mighty trees
>> home for birds
>>> in harmony they dwelt
>>> symphony unmatched.

Anteaters
Armadillos
Bears
Buffaloes
Cats
Caterpillars
Chameleons
Chimpanzees
Dogs
Donkeys
Elephants
Eagles
Giraffes
Horses
Hippos
Lions
Mice
Monkeys
Orangutans
Rhinos
Tigers
Zebras
All lived
in one family
in total peace.

continues

Paradise indeed.

No tears
No sickness
No weapons
No drugs
No sorrow
No death.

Pain
Anger
Malice
Bitterness
Greed
    unheard of.

Peace so perfect
Joy so complete.

Evening came.
Elohim came
    for His evening walk
    with Adam and Eve
    they talked and laughed
    shared their joy
    untouched by self.

Adam and Eve
    reigned over the earth
    unlimited power
        in mind and soul.
God gave them authority to rule
    the entire earth
    Garden of Eden
    Paradise.

Then one day
    Eve strolled out alone
    for a morning walk.
"Where are you going?"
    Adam asked.
This she never did before,
    going alone.
    Adam was puzzled.
"She wants to be alone;
    let it be,"
    he said to himself.

The devil made a bargain
    with the snake
"I will make you a god
    if you talk for me."
And so he did.

continues

Controlled by Satan
        the snake talked to Eve
        as she strolled along
        in the Garden alone
"Eve, look at this fruit
        so tasty, so fresh.
        Pluck and eat.
        You will like it."

"Oh, no,
        I can't do that
        for God said
        not to eat that fruit,"
                Eve replied.

"Don't be fooled by God, Eve."
        The snake talked
                with a convincing look.
"You will become like God
        if you eat this fruit.
        That is why God told you
                not to eat it.
                He is selfish."

She looked around
    and with trembling hands
    she plucked the fruit
    forbidden by God.

She bit into it
    died inside
    and lost her innocence.

All is lost.

She ran back to Adam
    shaking and trembling
    holding the rest
    of the fruit in her hand.

"What have you done?"
    Adam asked.
She didn't have to say
    He knew it all.

Now he must choose
    to live in Paradise
    or to sin and lose all
        to be cut off from God's life!

continues

For the love of a woman
    he chose.
He opened his arms
    embraced her
    her head resting on his shoulder
    she held him tight.
He took the fruit
    bit into it
    chose to die.
Full of shame
    guilt
    lost innocence
    naked
They looked for cover.

Evening came.
Elohim came
    to walk with them.
    They couldn't be found.

"Where are you?"
God asked.

"We have sinned,
    and we have hidden away
    from your face!"

continues

God was grieved
    He loved them so much
His children
    separated from Him
    by sin.
Now they would know
    sickness and sorrow
    pain and agony
    tears and hurt
    death and separation.

Hand in hand
    Adam and Eve walked out
        through the gate
    their backs to God
    to suffer and die.

Paradise lost.

God stood still
    deeply hurt.
He said to Himself,
    "Some day
    I will
    see them
    again."

Temptation

The line is thrown
    with the bait on the hook
    by the fishermen
    to catch a fish.

The hook and the bait
    are custom made
    for the kind of fish
    he wants to trap.

There is pleasure in sin
    for a season at least
    if you go for the pleasure
    you are caught with a hook.

Temptation is the bait
    demons cast
    death awaits you—
    flee for life.

Decision

Emotions were stirred
thoughts began to flow
    will said, "think"
    feelings said, "me."

Decision was made
action was done
    result was tragic
    it all began with a thought.

God's Book says
to guard your mind
    for out of it come
    the issues of life.

Be Strong

Demons from hell
    out there to fight
    to tear you up
and all that you have.

Stand your ground
    they may be strong
    but you are stronger
like David of old.

Satan is defeated
    with all his hosts
    by Christ on the cross
and you are in Christ.

Enable Me

Enable me, Jesus,
>to build faith for someone
>to give hope to the hopeless
>to create confidence
>to generate enthusiasm
>to spread peace
>to turn dreams to reality
>to turn problems into opportunities
>to lift up the fallen
>to bind up the hurting
>to say a kind word
>to let someone lean on me
>to find joy in serving

and thus
>I may become more like You.

Amen.

Listen

Spider had her lunch
    with the last fly she trapped;
then she cleaned her house
    to avoid suspicion
    from her next victim.

Moments later
    a fly buzzed by her web.
Spider called out,
    "Come on over, fly.
    Let's have a chat."

"No," said fly,
    as he steered to one side
    of the web.

There below,
    he saw thousands of flies
    dancing on the ground.
He wanted to go
    and dance with them.

Bee flew by
and said to the fly,
    "Don't you land there;
    you will die."

continues

"Go your way,
        stinging Bee.
I know my people.
They are having fun
        dancing down there."

Bee flew away.
The fly circled
        and began to land.
It was a trap.

What will it profit
to try to escape Spider's trap
        but land on a glue pad
        and end your life?

Listen to God's Word;
Though it may sting you much,
        it is the only way to
        live a full life.

Ship in Time

> Luxury liner
> sailed away
> with hundreds
> who boarded
> to enjoy life.
>
> Days on end
> of fantasies fulfilled
> with drink
> women
> laughter and all.
>
> Entertainment unlimited
> twenty-four hours
> "This is heaven,"
> one passenger said.
>
> Out in the ocean
> the ship sailed along
> two weeks to go until
> they reached the next port.

continues

Then disaster struck
    the ship hit an iceberg
    made a hole
    in the bottom of the ship.

The captain knew
    how dangerous it was;
    just like the Titanic
    they would soon sink.

He got on the speaker
    and announced to all,
    "Drink, be merry
    and enjoy life.

"Everything is free
    for everyone now.
    Take all you want
    hold nothing back."

In a few hours
    the ship sank
    to the bottom of the ocean
    All died.

The world is a ship
        sailing in the ocean of time
        time is running out
        it will all be burned up.

Devil,
        the god of this world, says,
        "Have fun now
        and all you want."

Don't be fooled,
        dear friend,
        it is not worth
        living for passing sin.

Blind Man

They walk along
without light.
They need none
for they are blind.

They stumble and fall
along the way
going where
they do not know.

They are blinded
by demons from hell.
They wander around
without hope.

Jesus came to open
these blind ones' eyes.
All they need to do
is call upon Him.

Doom is near
time is running out.
Cry out to Jesus
Say, "Lord Jesus, save me now."

When I Am Afraid

When the child was five
He became very ill—
"Surgery a must."
Parents were sad.

" 'When I am afraid
I will trust in You.'
Say it with me,"
The mother told her little one.

Before they put the mask on him
His mother bent down
And whispered in his ear,
" 'When I am afraid . . .'
      —keep saying this in your heart."

Surgery is over.
Now for twenty-four hours
His body remains paralyzed—
But inside, alert.

Fear grips the child
During this time.
He wants to scream
But can't say a word.

continues

Like a nightmare,
paralyzed with fear;
He wants to cry for help
But can't do a thing.

Results of this are all
Quite unnerving.
Children often become
Troubled, with restless minds.

As he was waking up
His first words were,
"When I am afraid, I will trust in You."
A happy and contented smile spread over his face.

"Mummy, I was so scared," he said.
"I wanted to scream,
I could not even blink my eyes.
It was really bad."

"Then I began saying in my heart,
'When I am afraid, I will trust in You'
And I felt as though Jesus was there
And I wasn't afraid anymore."

All of us face times like these—
Abandoned by all
Alone in our world
When no one can help.

God's unchanging promise
Is given to you.
Keep saying it in your heart:
"When I am afraid, I will trust in You."

"When I am afraid, I will trust in You."

—Psalm 56:3, NKJV, Bible

Flood That Killed

What if you and I were standing beside Noah when God talked
to him and gave him the plans, when the doors were shut and the
heavens cried? What was it really like?

It was the worst of times.

Evil filled the earth
Total anarchy reigned
Only the most
    vicious
    wicked
    brutal
    unkind
    selfish
    cruel
could survive
So bad it was.

God looked down from His throne
a cloud of wickedness covered the earth
His heart was grieved
    felt sad
for creating man
    in His image
    with free will.

"What must be done
	must be done."
He said to Himself
No turning back.

Mighty angel was summoned
before the throne.
	"Go and search the earth
	to see if there is anyone
		even one person
	righteous in heart."

Report came back
about Noah
who stayed true
to the Living God.

God came down
	to talk with Noah
	about His plan
	to judge the world.

Noah listened
	about a flood
	about to come
	upon the earth.

continues

Noah cried out
for mercy
on behalf of
all mankind.

"Please, God,
give more time!
They might repent
and change their ways."

"All right, Noah.
I will give you
one hundred twenty years
to warn them all.

"Meanwhile
you must build a boat
to save yourself and
your family."

"Boat?
What is that, God?"

"It is a house
that will float on water
all made of wood.
Here are the blueprints.
Make sure you build
according to this plan
in every detail."

Righteous Noah
began to preach
about a flood
that would come.

His sons were engaged
in cutting down trees
to build the ark
as God had said.

He employed
many skilled men
carpenters and all
to get the boat built.
    The workmen
    mocked and laughed at Noah
    and the flood
    he preached about.

continues

"What is rain, man?"
one joked.
"Flood? Whoever heard of that?"
another laughed.

"Hey, be quiet,"
said a third.
"He is mad,
we all know that.
Let him be,
     just as long as we get
     our pay."

So they went on
building the ark
     joking and
     laughing about
     the ark.

Few were truly concerned
about what Noah was saying
     most thought he had gone mad
     in his mind.

As the years went by
nothing seemed to happen
     Everyone was convinced
     it was all a sham.

They drank much more
made others drink
building
selling
buying
letting the good times roll.

One hundred twenty years
came to an end.
The ark was finished.
Time ran out.

No one had repented.
No one had believed.
No one had cared.
No one had cried.

"Noah, listen,"
God said,
"Take a pair of
every kind of animal
into the ark.
All birds and bees
also must go in.

continues

"You too
go in
with your family.
It is time to
close the door."

Like any other day
        this day began—
People laughing
jesting everywhere.

"Where is he?"
someone asked.
"Oh, now he is in the
ark hiding from us!"

Earth groaned with pain
        quiet inside.
Trees stood numbed
        in agony.
Creation stopped
        breathing.
Not a trace of breeze
        to be found anywhere.
Beginning of the end
        all so strange.
Sound of silence
        heard everywhere.

God turned off the lights
Sun went to sleep
Not a star to be seen
    Dark clouds engulfed the earth
Thunder rolled
Lightning shot out
Rain began to fall
    Endlessly
    Ceaselessly.

Ark began to float
    men and women
    cried from outside
    beating their chest.

Water came up
    knee high
    waist high
    neck high
        kept rising
        kept rising
No letting up.

Beating on
    the side of the ark
they screamed,
    "Please, Noah, open!
    We repent!"

continues

"We helped you build this ark,"
    carpenters cried.
"Please open or
we all will die!"

"God has shut the door
    from without.
We can't do a thing.
    It is too late."

Monkeys climbed tall trees
    to find safety
Men followed after
    climbing trees.

Mothers climbed
    with infants in their arms,
each one fighting
for their lives.

Water kept rising
    over all trees
    mountains and hills.
Everything.

continues

DANCE NOT FOR TIME

The whole earth was
covered under water.
Not one living thing
survived.

The ark floated
        for forty days.
Finally the rain stopped
        and the flood went down.

At last
the ark rested on dry land
        on the side of a mountain
        called Ararat.

There in modern Turkey
on the top of Mount Ararat
        the ark of Noah
        rests in peace.
It sits there
reminding us
        the judgment of God
        will come on the earth
        as it did in Noah's time.

CRY
NO MORE

When I Was Young

Narrow winding paths
Golden paddy fields
Summer time
Harvest time.
Children
    flying kites
    running naked
    climbing trees
    picking fruits
    playing hide-and-seek
    I too.

I remember
the way it was
in my village
when I was young.

Summer
    came to an end
I was sad
    for school would soon start.
I had to go
    a mile away
    from my home.

Walking each day
    barefooted
    to the kindergarten
    to a half-naked teacher
    to learn the alphabet
    and to count numbers.
We sat on the dirt floor
With my finger
    I wrote in the sand
        Aa, Aaa, Ee, Eee
        Onne, Rande, Munne

And that
is the way it was
in my village
when I was young.

Everyone knew
    everyone else
    like a big family
    helping each other
    in time of need.
Loving folks
innocent
cared for others
taking risks.

continues

And that
is the way it was
in my village
when I was young.

No roads
    no street lights
    no police station
    of course no liquor shops
    drugs were unknown
    drunkards were outcasts
    wife beating was a shame
    young people didn't smoke.
We respected teachers
    and old folks alike.

And that
is the way it was
in my village
when I was young.

As the sun went to sleep
     kerosene lamps
          lit up the whole village
          like a starry night.
Evening time
     family prayer time
     singing and praying.
One could hear it
     from every house
     and tiny hut.

And that
is the way it was
in my village
when I was young.

When someone died
     the whole village
          felt the pain.
Most cried
     in the crowded house
     of the dead.
Times have changed
     everything has changed

continues

Now
    only a few come
    they talk and laugh
    in the house of the dead
and I wonder
what happened to
feelings anymore.

And it is no longer
the way it was
in my village
when I was young.

Liquor shops
    are a common sight
drunks in public
    stumble along.

Criminals roam the streets
    without fear
while common folks
    live in fear.
For the law
    doesn't punish
    the guilty anymore.

And it is not
the way it was

in my village
when I was young.

Students
      in politics
Most fail in studies
      and in life alike.

From the top
      orders come
            to strike in public
            to burn buses
            to stop trains
            provoke police
            let a few get killed
            or at least get beaten.
These innocent lambs
      sacrificed on the altar of greed
      by corrupt politicians
            to secure their power
      while their own children
      study abroad.

And it is not
the way it was
in my village
when I was young.

continues

Megatons of poison
     dumped into our fields
     washed into rivers
     killing all fish.

Bribes ensure that the corruption
     continues on
not even the media
ever talk about this crime.
Environment
     is destroyed
Look around
     if you will
What kind of future
     will your children
     and grandchildren have?

And it is not
the way it was
in my village
when I was young.

Roads
Street lights
Cars and bikes
Running water
TV, VCR

Telephone
Telefax
Telegram
Computers
Microwave

English-medium schools
Children, only four years old,
    in uniforms
    each one carrying
    armloads of books
    running for school bus
       and away from their childhood
Removed from nature
    sand dunes
    butterflies
    picking fruits
    frogs and ponds
Unaware they are
    children turned to adults.
Now we have it all
    and it all has made
       our lives so complicated
Each one cares
    for no one else
Our hearts
    have turned to stones.

continues

Old people
>> now a burden
>> lonely and forgotten
>> sit in a corner
>> they wish to die
So do their children
>> for no one has time
for anyone anymore.
How it all happened
I don't know.

But it is not
the way it was
in my village
when I was young.

Two weeks ago
>> a man killed
>> a man
>> with a dagger
>> while others watched.
They say
>> he was drunk
>> stabbed his friend
>> and all that happened
>> from a quarrel
>> over a five rupee note.

And I ask
    how come
    he is still free
    to go free?

The truth
    is too painful
The politicians
    and police
    for the bribe they received
    let him go
    free.
The church
    is sleeping
    in the light
They have forgotten
    to pray
    for the land.
While the innocent
    weep
    day and night
    in their huts
    no one cares
    no one weeps.
I cry with a few.

continues

Questions are many
    answers are few
Where will it all end?
I know it must.

And it is not
the way it was
in my village
when I was young.

The sun sets
in the morning
    empty homes
    empty faces
    greedy eyes
    lazy workers
        trying to make
        more money
        any way they can
        no matter
        who gets hurt.

Evening comes
Family prayers
    replaced with
    TV and VCR
    and sounds of silence.

Street lights
        illumine the village
        for an empty people
        with hearts of stone
        who live in the dark.

And it is not
the way it was
in my village
when I was young.

Take note
        you praying folks
        police and politicians
I plead with you
        to let Christ
        change your life
To do all you can
        to save this village
        before it is too late.

And oh,
how I wish
it would be
the way it was
in my village
when I was young.

Unhealthy Home

Everybody talking
No one listens.
Everybody wants to receive
No one wants to give.

Everybody wants to be served
No one wants to serve.
Everybody fights for their rights
No one wants to give in.

Everybody is right
No one admits he is wrong.
Everybody demands attention
No one wants to go unnoticed.

Everybody wants their rest and ease
No one wants responsibility.
Everybody wants everything right.
No one wants to pay the price.

If You Knew

My close friend
If you knew me
as I know me
You would not want
to be my friend ever again.

Things I did
Things I said
Things I didn't do
So many things . . .
More than you know.
I am so sorry
I weep
for hurting you
in a thousand ways.
Some you know
the rest you don't—
I am glad.

I regret
I repent
Dear Jesus,
Please forgive me.
He did.
I am new.
Amen.

In Satan's Kingdom

Drunk on skid row
Homicide
Electric chair
Jail
Death
Anger out of control
Dagger
Drugs and pain
Empty heart
Betrayed
No mercy
Hit-and-run
Liquor shop
Broken homes
Divorce
Runaway
Prodigal son
Pride and anger
Wars
Sadism
Voodoo
Witchcraft
Stealing
Lying

Adultery
Idol worship
Enemy
Selfishness
Suicide
Lost sheep
Darkness
Hell
Bitterness
Hopelessness
Fear of death

Safe

Cobra was mad
>tensions were high
>reapers fled the field
>fearing it would bite.

A mongoose saw the scene
>came to the spot
>he could not tackle the snake
>for it was a king cobra.

He circled the snake
>and sprayed his scent
>now the snake would not
>go out of the ring.

With lightning swiftness
>the mongoose sped away
>to call the king mongoose
>who would surely kill the snake.

Here came the king
>riding on the top
>of the mongoose
>who brought the news.

Although he was king,
    in his size he was small
    almost half of the size
    of the rest of the gang.

He surveyed the spot
    circled it twice
    took one leap
    the snake's head was gone.

The job was done
    he got on the back
    of the mongoose
    and went back home.

Satan is mad
    we are not his match
    Jesus is the King
    bruised his head
Now you are safe.

Fatal Words

A long time ago
in the north of the land
was a valley so steep
and full of trees.

A flock of birds
lived in them;
happy were they
and undisturbed.

A wedding day
for two young birds;
the whole flock came to
wish them well.

Happily married
they flew away,
side by side
to a tree of their own.

They built a home
at the top of the tree;
she gave birth
to five little ones.

As time moved on
they lost their love;
argued daily
over every little thing.

He started drinking
with his friends;
came home late
and didn't care anymore.

Then one day
the fight broke out;
in a frenzy,
they plucked
the nest apart
inch
by
inch.

continues

Their featherless children
fell to the ground
with painful cries,
died instantly.
The sun had set,
clouds covered the sky
and not a star would smile.

They flew away
into the night
without a word.
Words destroyed their home.

Orphan Boy

His father was sick, and they were poor.
They went to the hospital that was government run.
Waiting for days in the open veranda
Hoping to find someone who would help.

The twelve-year-old son had lost a week's school
Now, half-starving, sitting with his dad.
Last year his mother died on the same spot
They say she died for lack of bribe.

Finally, his father cries,
"Please, dear God, let me die."
Wiping his tears, the boy went to a doctor
Knelt at his feet and begged for his dad.

"What can I do?" the doctor replied.
"You go and get this medicine for him."
Without wasting a moment, the boy ran to the shop
Pleaded, "Please, we are poor—help my father live."

continues

The shopkeeper turned his face away
The boy, with his head down, walked slowly back
Called to his father, who seemed asleep
But though he called again and again,
    there was no reply.

Now he is alone in this wide world
Corruption and bribe killed his father
How many millions must die like him
Before we wake up and change the system?

Dalit

Crowded railway stations
Crowded streets
Garbage heaps
    search for food

Tens of thousands
Little kids
Lonely and hungry
    Everywhere.

If they wish to run away
Where can they go anyway?

Waking up each morning
To the cold streets
With rumbling stomachs
    no money to buy food.

Cry No More

The pain you feel,
The burden you bear,
    no one knows
    no one understands.

Things you can't change
Though you've often tried—
    all is dark
    hope is lost.

All you want is life to end.

Cry no more, my dear friend
Come to Christ—
He will make all things new.

Prayer

Your holy presence
my spirit longs for
but my flesh rebels
    Kyrie-Eleison.*

Memories of duties neglected
prompting of your Spirit
ignored and disobeyed
    Kyrie-Eleison.*

When the poor and needy
knocked at my door
now I know it was You
    Kyrie-Eleison.

Thank You for grace
mercy and forgiveness
Here I am on my knees
    Kyrie-Eleison.

*Greek: *Lord, have mercy.*

Promise

When you feel
    lonely
    sad and hurt

May you hear
    His gentle voice
    speaking to you

"I will never
    leave you nor
    forsake you
    until your journey
    comes to an end."

I WILL

NEVER

LEAVE YOU

Beggar Girl

One late afternoon, on Bombay's street
I walked alone to meet a friend
There was a street I had to cross
I waited for the light, with many like me.

Children crowded all around me
Stretched out their arms begging for help
I have known this scene a million times
I told myself to look angry and mean.

Pathetic cries came from everywhere
I said to myself, "It is all a fake.
Don't give a penny; they are only cheats.
Keep your eyes fixed on your light."

Dozens of mothers carrying children
Skinny and naked with bloated stomachs
Only one look would break any heart
And I didn't want to face that reality.

Suddenly I heard a sad, gentle voice
From behind me—it pierced through my being,
"Sir, my father died from TB
My mother cannot beg, she is very ill.

"I have three young children who are crying
Please give me a few pennies to buy some food."
The light turned green and then red again
But I could not move, for I was in shock.

continues

Dance Not for Time

I turned around to see her face
I was stunned by the sheer beauty I saw
Barely nine, with big brown eyes
Long black hair fell below her knees.

Uncared for, unwashed, unkempt for months
Dirt mingled with sweat ran down her face.
Her skin was fair, one could see,
But the rag she wore was dirty and black.

There she stood with hands stretched out
I could not take my eyes from her face
Gave her money, more than she hoped
I walked away, but not quite alone.

All of a sudden, a stranger appeared
And began to walk and talk with me.
"What do you think of that beggar girl?" he asked.
I thought about all I had just experienced.

In my mind's eye I saw the girl again
And standing with her, another girl, just about nine
The beggar girl's name I did not know
The other little one—I knew her well.

continues

That little girl is my daughter Sarah
Happy and beautiful and liked by all
Has her own room with nice little things,
Parents to love her and Jesus she loves.

"What is the worth of this street girl, my friend?"
Asked the stranger gently again.
I responded,
    "Her life is, of course, worth as much as mine."
"What is that to you?" the stranger asked.

I walked alone again, pondering it all
My heart was heavy and my eyes were wet.
Once again I vowed to myself
To reach out and touch others in need.

If They

If they said things
about you
Which you say
about others

If they thought evil
about you
The way you think
about others

If they misunderstood
you
The way you misunderstand
others

If they gossiped
about you
The way you gossip
about others

If they cheated
you
The way you cheat
others

continues

If they lied
	about you
The way you lie
	about others

If they were unkind
	to you
The way you are unkind
	to others

If they didn't forgive and forget
	your wrongs
The way you refuse to forgive and forget
	others

If they hated
	you
The way you hate
	others

If they were greedy
	at your time of need
As you are greedy
	when faced with others' needs

If others knew
    your life
The way you know
    yourself

If God treated
    you
The way you treat
    others

Where would you be today?
What would you deserve?
How would you feel?
What are your thoughts now?
How would you change?

Will you change?

"Do unto others
What you would have others do to you."

        —Jesus

Happiness Is . . .

A close friend
Someone to love
A house to live in
To be appreciated
A loving husband
A gentle wife
Children who mind

An enjoyable job
A boss who is human
Hearing the words, "Thank you"

A good sermon
Good neighbors
A loving dog
Mild weather
Good health

Smiling often
Laughing much

Enjoying others' success
Meeting sincere people

Someone you trust
Knowing a good mechanic
Finding a good doctor

A church that loves
A pastor who teaches
Being healed by a touch of God

Good books
Soft music
An old clock that works

A clean house
A train that is on time
An uncrowded bus

Rain when needed
A nice garden with flowers
Healthy children
The ability to enjoy nature

continues

A shortwave radio to hear world news
Having a bicycle
Having a two-wheeler
Having a car

A wife who doesn't nag
A husband who says, "I love you"

Money to meet needs
A clear starry night
Seeing the big picture
Someone who encourages you when you are down
Quitting a bad habit
Traveling in a reserved compartment in the train
Being paid well for a job well done

Having loyal workers
Having loyal friends
Having your sins forgiven.

It Is a Girl

She cried out loud that night she was born
Her parents cried also, for it was a girl.
"I told you to abort it!" her husband chided.
"It is all her fault," his parents said.

Is there more sorrow than to be born a woman
In India, a land where goddesses reign?
From the day she is born till the day she dies
The sound of her agony is heard everywhere.

Dowry deaths escalate day by day
No one seems to care for the women in this land.
Many fought for freedom and died for their country
Who will now fight for the women to free her at last?

God made both man and woman in His image
He gave them life and worth equally
Religions that treat women so low—I reject
Christ came to give dignity to women
        just as He did men.

Can you feel the pain of the women in this land?
Do something to give them their rights
Man, how can you hate them so much?
For it was a woman who gave you life.

Who Cares for Her?

She works on the road, breaking up stones
Carries them on her head to the men on the job
From morning till night she toils and labors
What she receives are abuse and pain.

Her long black hair is unkempt and unwashed
Her clothes are old and full of holes
Her big brown eyes tell stories of pain
Her back is bent from carrying the loads.

The heat of the sun bakes her skin
She was once fair, but now black and leathery
Her husband is at the liquor shop drinking his brew
Her children wander naked on the streets.

The sun has set and her agony starts
She trembles with the thought of going home
It is no house, only a shanty in the slums
She wouldn't mind if she had a family that cared.

She walks in with the food she has bought
At midnight he comes, roaring as a beast
Shouting and screaming and calling her names
She runs and hides, like a mouse from the cat.

The ordeal will last until nearly dawn
Finally he sleeps and she has peace
The children cried themselves to sleep hours before
Now she wishes she never was born.

Come look through the window of her face, my friend
Millions like her die a very slow death
Not only in slums, but in mansions and everywhere
Because no one cares for these precious lives.

Do you, my friend, care for your wife?
Love her now, with all that you are
Don't break her heart, for she trusts in you
When all is gone, she will be the only thing you have.

How Lonely Life Can Be

It is late, he is not home
And when he is, he barely talks.
The children are in bed and she is alone
Again she will cry herself to sleep.

When he came home, she did not know
Early in the morning she makes his tea.
Newspaper comes to bury his face
She sits next to him, but he never sees.

He leaves again to his daily work
Leaves her alone to face her depression.
The children are in school and she is alone
In a home where the telephone never rings.

The postman goes by—no letters for her
The neighbors come to borrow something.
The hours drag on, yet there's much to be done
This day is the same as any other.

"I am alone, oh God," she cries.
"Please do something to ease this pain!"

The answer comes back from Calvary's mount,
"I suffered alone so your heart can be filled."

He Is There

When you need answers to facts or feelings,
    He is there.
When you need a shoulder to lean on,
    He is there.
When you hear voices
causing more confusion than peace,
    He is there.
When you are all alone
and the sound of silence is your company,
    He is there.
When work is piled up
and you can't see how it all could be done,
    He is there.
When no one notices the labor you put in,
when you feel unappreciated,
    He is there.
When you need someone just to talk to
and can't find anyone,
    He is there.

"I will never leave you
nor forsake you."

    —Jesus

Divine Embrace

The wonder of the
    rugged log
stained with blood
    of the God-Man
transcends time and space
like none other in history.

There on the cross
He stretched out His arms
    of love and grace
    of divine embrace
for the lost and damned
sinners like us.

He, the divine love,
invites us, His followers,
    to be His loving arms
    to stretch out our arms
    to be the divine embrace
for the wandering souls.

Change our hearts, O Spirit of God,
fill us with the love of Christ
    consume us within
    to completely be Your
    outstretched arms
        of divine embrace.

Smile Again

How can it be
　　I ask
It was bright and warm

But without any warming
　　Sun went to sleep
It is cold and so dark

Can you tell me, please
Where do I find shelter?
　　It is so cold
So alone I feel.

Darkness I fear
Which way I must take?
Will the sun rise again?
If so
How long must I wait?

My strength is spent
　　Emotions dry.

I wish I knew what must I do
To find hope and
　　Smile again.

I Hope

I hope my friendship
    edged you along
    to love Him more dearly
    who loves you so much.

I hope my prayers
    kept you safe
    in raging storms
    and in times of despair.

I hope my faith in you
    encouraged you
    to stay in the battle
    no matter how hard it was.

I hope you know my love for you
    wishing God's best
    always for you
    in all your ways.

Nobody

In thinking about the Dalits of India and the suffering
they so often experience in their lives, I began to ask
myself: What if that were me?

I am nobody
Worthless my life is
To Untouchables I was born.
A Dalit child my fate sealed.

I was born in slums
Rights? We have none
To upper-caste our lives we owe
Slaves to serve all their wish

Poverty and hunger
Is all I ever knew
If there is hope
Tell me how?

What is my future?
Do I have any?
It all looks so dark
And I wish I was not born.

Life without God Is . . .

Dried-up lake
Artist without brush
Pen without ink
Moon without sun
Lifeless body
Slavery
Sail without wind
Shepherdless flock.

Blank page
Clouds without rain
Tree without fruit
Dead fish in the stream
Aimless drifting
Endless night.

One Star

It is late
I am alone
In my room
Far away
from my home.

No phone to ring
No one to visit
My door is locked
It is dark.

I get up
Walk to the window
Stand by it
And stare at the sky.

Silent night
Stars shimmer
Then clouds move in
To cover their beauty.

Through the clouds
One star smiles
Whispers to my heart,

continues

"I am the star
That led the shepherds
To the manger
In Bethlehem."

Emmanuel
Lamb of God
Slain for me
Rose again
He is here
With me now
I am not alone
Never will be.

LIFT
UP
YOUR
EYES

More Important

A two-story mansion
    was their home
Rich in affluence
    they had all in this world
Servants they had
    to do everything.

Occasionally beggars came
    asking for help.
One day a blind beggar
    came by the gate
        with his wife
        holding his hand.
He got some help
    and they walked away
        still talking and laughing
        holding hands.

The lady of this home
    saw them from an upper room
Through the window
    she stood, gazing at them.

"I wish I could trade
    places with her;
    I am so lonely,"
she said to herself.

What is the use
    if you gain the whole world
        but there is no one to love
        and no one loves you?

The lesson is obvious
    even to the blind
People are more important
    than anything else.

Street Light and the Boy

One late night on a downtown street,
A young boy sat by the road.
The street light above him shone brightly—
The boy was studying his books from school.

I watched from a distance and asked myself,
"Is he a street boy without a home?
What about his parents, is he alone?"
I walked slowly to the rusty lamp post.

"What is your name, young friend?" I asked.
He only stared, and wouldn't say a word.
I sat down next to him and told him my name.
Then again I asked for his name and age.

He said he was twelve, without a home.
His parents were beggars. His name was Ashok.
He went to school during the day,
And at night studied under this light.

"Some day it will all change," he spoke with hope.

In his eyes I saw millions in despair—
Their lives are as precious as yours and mine.
But knowing this truth will not change one thing
Find your own Ashok, for there are many out there.

One Smile

Bucket full
    water was cold
    to take a bath
I was freezing.

Opened the red tap
    hot water came
    in a few seconds
cold turned warm.

One smile
    one kind word
    a loving touch
will give warmth to others.

Tell Me Why

I've seen the suffering of the Dalits. I've heard their cries as I've read their stories. I wrote this poem as I contemplated their anguish.

Tell me why
gods hate us so much
won't let us in their temples
to talk to them.

Tell me why
High-caste despise us
yet without our servitude
they can't survive.

Tell me why
we are forbidden
to draw water from a well
by upper-caste whom we serve.

Tell me why
it took 3,000 years
for our eyes to open
to the curse of casteism
that made us slaves.

Tell me why
Mr. High-caste, tell me why
we should not quit this cursed system
to find hope in "Jeeshu"
who came to set us free?

There Is More

There is more to life than you ever thought
Thinking "this is the end" is not truly so
You are not alone in this big world
It is full of hurting people who need your help.

There is a rich man, dying alone.
A mother who has lost her child grieves alone.
A wife who has a drunk for a husband weeps alone.
A child who lost his parents walks alone.

It is in giving that our needs are met.
Weep for others and you shall find joy
Touch someone to live again
Your life is too short to sit alone.

Look at what you have, if you will
Legs to walk, hands to work
Eyes to see beauty and ears to hear
Someone who loves you more than you know.

Think of the blind man who stumbles and falls
The deaf who can't hear the sounds of love
The cripple who begs on the side of the road
The millions who cry for a touch of love.

Lift up your eyes and look away
From your world that is so tiny and small
Hear their cries—and please walk with me
Let us give our lives that they may live.

You Be My Jesus

The night is darker than the darkest night
not a star in the sky.
Cruel storm howls in distance
    creating piercing silence.
Non-stop downpour.
It seems this night is forever.

My lamp is empty
    only left the smoking wick
    hurting my eyes
forcing me to shut them in the dark.

Is there anyone who cares
    to understand
to say a kind word
    to lend a helping hand?
Yes, I know Jesus cares
Jesus understands.

But I don't see Him
       can't touch Him
       Where is He?

Till I find Him
Please stay with me
Please take my hand

It is so dark
YOU BE MY JESUS
I am all alone.
       Alone.

Child of a Slum

An innocent child
    so weak and small
    helpless and defenseless
born in Dharavi slum.

She is three years old
    not even a rag she has
    to cover her fragile body
so many like her.

Her toys are made of mud and stones
when hungry she eats grass and dirt.
Her father a drunk and drug addict
nobody knows where he is.

Her mother left her and her siblings
to fend for themselves in the slums.
It is late evening before she returns
with money she got from begging on streets.

How many precious children
      suffer like this and worse
            and what is their future
If we don't care?

How does one bring hope
to such horrible suffering?
The answer is plain—
if we choose to obey the Word of God.

Yes, millions in the slums cry for help.
We are the answer to their prayers.
See Jesus in the little ones
      and do all we can
            to give them life.

Bring Them

I heard about a dog
who was hit by a car
  driven by a doctor
  on his way to work.

Stopping the car,
he got out and saw
  the whining dog
  with a broken leg.

He took the dog with him
to his clinic nearby
  bound up the wound
  gave some food.

In a few weeks
the dog was well.

Now it became a custom
for the dog to visit
  the doctor at work and
  they became friends.

A few months later,
the doctor heard a scratch
    from the rear door
    of his clinic.

He opened the door
and saw his friend
    who brought a dog
    with a broken leg.

From the look in his eyes
the doctor knew the tale:
    he had brought his friend
    to get him well.

You have been made whole
by the Master's touch;
    now go find the hurting
    and bring them to Christ.

Vendor of Sticks

I heard the story of a little boy in one of our Bridge of Hope centers who had lost his mother to hard labor. I remember feeling his hurt and wrote this poem at the time.

Dark, skinny body—this was my mother
Eyes sunken with pain
Turns and looks at us
As she disappears into the woods.

It is late in the afternoon
We children had eaten nothing all day
Waiting and watching for mother
After selling the sticks to come home with food.

Our father left for a neighboring state
Looking for a coolie's job
For Untouchables here like us
There is no job except cleaning latrines.

Poverty and hunger took their toll
My mother died without help
My brothers and I did not know what to do
Wandering on streets all day long.

Our father came home a broken man
Held us in his arms crying bitterly
He sits and gazes into the dark
Mutters to himself I don't know what.

The sun rose with bright hope
Some kind people took us to school
At first I didn't know much at all
Now I know we have hope.

Often my eyes seek my mother
I still cry and grieve
When I see a dark skinny vendor of wood
I wish I had money to buy her sticks.

Walked Alone

Have you noticed how sad they look
Old or young—they care for none
Each one walks as if alone.

Are you alone on this crowded street?
The sound you hear is your heart beat
No one to talk to for you see none.

I, too, walked alone, as you do now
Then one day I stood still, by the road
And saw the many, just like me.

Blinded by my own ego, I couldn't see
That I was far better off than many out there.
Others became my concern from then on;
It was no longer me alone.

To think of others and their hurts,
Giving my life away for others in need
This was the way I found my life.

You Can

Don't say
You can't

You can
I know

Not in
Your strength but
By His grace.

Modern Prodigal

There was a young man, from the south of the land
His father, a kind farmer was he
The boy was stubborn and rebellious
His friends were nothing but bad company.

He took all the money that he could get
And ran off to Bombay—the big city
Before the train even arrived
He had friends, and plenty of them.

Together they sauntered into town
To enjoy the life of his dreams
Movies, women, drugs, gambling and all
He hardly had time to sleep at night.

Finally he found himself penniless
His pockets were empty, and so was his heart
He felt lonely without his friends
But they had all left him, for now he was poor.

He knocked at many doors to find a place to sleep
No one would take him, for he had nothing
Forsaken, forgotten and destitute
He wandered on the streets, wishing to die.

One evening on the Chaupati beach
He met a man who gave him a book
That night he sat under the streetlight
And what he read changed his life.

The book was a portion from the Bible
In it he read about himself
The prodigal son was just like he was
Stinking and dirty and rejected by all.

That night he came to his senses and saw
The way out of his troubles was to come back to God
He repented of his ways and turned toward home
His father gladly welcomed him back.

Take It

He didn't take a bath
    for how long—who knows?
The stench from his body
    was worse than a skunk.

Soap and water
    were plentiful everywhere;
he could be clean
    but he just didn't care.

The blood of Jesus
    shed on the cross,
is a fountain to cleanse
    the vilest man.

Unless you take it
    to make your heart clean,
don't blame God—
    He has done all He must.

Winter Day

That winter day in Sri Nagar
The bitter cold chilled me to the bone
As usual I woke early that day
Put on my shawl and walked down the road.

Early in the morning the "chaia" man was up
I was so glad his shop was lit
I sat on the old bench and asked for my tea
The old man gave me my tea in a glass.

Now it was time to open the Word
Reading the portion while sipping my tea
The verse from Corinthians spoke to my heart:
"Henceforth I know no man after the flesh."

My eyes were opened to see his lost soul
I began to speak and tell of Jesus
His tea pan was boiling, but he didn't see
He sat transfixed by every word I said.

I saw his eyes wet with tears
He asked me to tell him more of His love
That day he asked Jesus to save him
I will never forget that winter day.

No Longer Alone

One shouldn't be lonely
    in a crowd like this
    but I was.

No one knew
    my world
    I lived alone
    with unending work
    but for His grace
    I would be sad.

Then one day
    you came along
    things changed
    I was no longer alone
    in the crowd
    in the battle.

You with me
    changed everything.

Thank you
    for praying
    for words of comfort
    for smiles
    and I bless you
    in Jesus' name.

YOU CAN

BE

FREE

Harvest Time

He was barely five
    walking with his dad
        who was a farmer
    through their wheat field.

It was almost harvest time
    golden wheat
        dancing on the wind
    all around them.

"Why, Dad,"
    the boy asks,
"are so many stalks standing up straight
while others bend down to the ground?"

"You see, my son,
the stalks that stand straight
    have no grain in them
    like the ones bent to the ground.

"It is only a matter of time
until the grainless ones
        will be fed to the flames
while the grain goes to the barn.

"There are people
just like this chaff.
    Learn from their end
    and refuse to be like them."

Only Strangers

He was a judge
Mighty in the land
He lived in a mansion
At the top of the hill.

He had servants
At every turn
A horse and buggy
Took him everywhere.

Hundreds worked
Like slaves every day
To build his house
With Burmese teak.

His gates were locked
His dogs, vicious guards
The poor and the beggars
He hated with contempt.

His wife died first
Then his daughter took the house
But not long after
She also died.

continues

The house sat still
For many years
Rats, snakes and bats
Make it their home.

His dream house is gone
His name is forgotten
Even his grandchildren left
For another land.

He forgot to remember
That the earth is the Lord's
And the fullness thereof
We are only strangers.

A Mystery

> I walked alone and asked myself,
> After I left her to cry alone,
> "Why do I hurt her, the one I love,
> More than anyone here on earth?"
>
> It is an irony I don't understand—
> We can be kind to strangers we've just met,
> But hurt the ones who love us the most.

No One to Help

There was an elephant
    big and tall
    despised by all
for he was mean.

Alone he roamed
    through the woods
    terror to all
shunned by all.

One day he fell into a ditch
    no one came to help
    weeks he cried
    became weak
died in solitude.

No one lives
    on an island alone
Live in such a way
    that you have friends.

A Cat's Advice

Tiger the dog was a German shepherd
Mickey the cat a furry one.
Romped and played, they ran around
Closest of friends in every way.

From morning till night, Tiger was in a cage
During the night he was free.
This was when they got together
To talk about the news of the day.

One morning when Mickey walked by the cage
Tiger was crying—buckets of tears.
Mickey was stunned, she went to the cage
Put her paws through bars, lay still and waited.

Tiger tried hard to hide his tears
It was too late—Mickey saw it all.
"Why are you crying, Tiger?" Mickey asked.
"You're usually such a brave one
        —I can't understand it."

Tiger wiped his tears and told his story
"Mickey, I wish I was born a cat.
You roam about free night and day
I sit in this cage which is worse than death.

continues

"Is it because I am a dog, do you think?
Am I not doing my job, to watch this house?
I am brave and bold—you know.
But all I get is mean treatment."

Mickey was touched by Tiger's words.
Lovingly and gently she told him,
"You can be free, Tiger, just like me,
If you can change your behavior a bit.

"Think of the times you attacked other dogs.
You ran with bad company and broke Master's heart.
One time, your leg was broken by boys
Only because you wouldn't let them alone.

"Your behavior has alienated you from all
Now people think you are mean and tough.
If only you can be more loving
Don't put on a show to try to prove anything.

"It is not by hating that you gain;
Love others and you shall be loved.
With this change in mind, I am sure
You can be free just like me."

What Went Wrong?

A story is told by someone I know,
About a rich man in his village and his greedy soul.

The patriarch of the family was over eighty-five then;
Landlords who owned and controlled much land.

The man had four sons to boast of his fame;
Like a king on the hill with them he reigned.

Their laborers were treated cruelly by them—
Beaten—their wages held back by these powerful men.

The poor workers' children cried at night for food;
Their parents would feed them, if only they could.

Time moved on, and nothing stayed the same;
All good things, they say, must come to an end.

Thirty years passed; the king on his hill is gone.
But his grandchildren beg for food all day long.

You may ask, "What went wrong, why this sad end?"
The lesson is this—I'll tell you, my friend:

Don't build your wealth on the tears of the poor;
For one day their tears may well become yours.

Mean Couple

I want to tell you about a couple
Who destroyed more lives than I can tell.
All over the world you find them for sure
Especially in our day they are easy to find.

The first murder in history was committed by Cain;
He killed his brother because of *envy*.
"Why must he be blessed more than I?" said he;
The power of envy can kill anyone.

Then, how many homes are torn apart
Because of *jealousy* among its members?
No one is happy for others' betterment.
They hate each other because of envy.

You do voodoo to hurt your neighbors,
To destroy their lives because of envy.
What you don't realize is that
        "you reap what you sow"—
In time, envy will destroy you too.

It is by blessing that you are blessed;
Job prayed for his enemies
        and in turn he was blessed.
Be happy for others' prosperity,
And you will be blessed
in ways you can't imagine.

Prison

He built a prison and sat within
Doors and gates were thickest steel
The lock was placed within the door
It was locked with a solitary key.

There were guards who tormented him
Day and night, he cried alone
The tormenters were seen by none
For they were demons from the unseen world.

His prison was built with unforgiveness
The hate he possessed locked him in
Wings to fly were torn apart
No one could help him, for he alone held the key.

I Killed My Enemy

He was an enemy of mine
for many long years.

The pain he inflicted
caused deep wounds
turned to bitterness
deep in my soul.

My stomach writhed
turned to ulcers.
The thought of his name
made me shrink.

Finally I read
the words of Jesus,
"Love your enemies
and bless them much."

I began to pray,
"God, please bless him
and his household
in all their ways."

The following week
    his birthday came
I sent him a card
    and a gift in the mail.

Went to see him
    that very week
I said, "I am sorry.
    I need you as my friend."
He didn't shake my hand
    instead hugged me tight
    his tears fell on my neck.

I killed my enemy
for now he is my friend.

Loggers

Loggers walked
in the woods
cutting down trees
to build a new home.

Logs were rolled
into the river
floating downstream
for days to the site.

Along the way
one log
    big and long
blocked the others
from going down the stream.

The workers came
    pushing and pulling
hoping it would
shift and move along
with the rest.

Nothing worked
no matter
        how much they tried
finally the order came
to blast it.

Holes were drilled
        into the log
dynamite put in place
switch turned on.

The blast was heard
        a mile away
now shredded in pieces
no more a log.

Your life is given
        to be a blessing
don't block others
from going on
        with life.

Dance Not for Time

The Well and the Seed

There was a well
I know so well
Its water was sweet
And a source of joy to all.

One day a crow
Came to the well
Sat on the rim
To eat its lunch.

One seed dropped
Into the well
From the bird's beak
And lodged in the wall.

Water and sun
Helped the seed sprout
It began to grow
And became an oak.

continues

Thick roots went through
The wall of the well
The walls soon crumbled—
Those roots killed the well.

No more sweet water
For all to enjoy
Now it is desolate
What a sad end.

Our heart is a well
With sweet water for all
But a root of bitterness
Can stop its flow.

Words

Words are seeds
With life in them.

What you sow
You will reap.

Confession

Mad as a mad dog
    he came at me
    to tear me up
    for what I said.

I'd repeated gossip
    which was told to me
    about this man
    by a friend of his.

Words of flame
    about to fly
    to burn me down
    when I said,
"It is my fault."

His mouth dropped
    he looked straight at me
    didn't say a word.
    I knew why.

"Please forgive me.
I have sinned,"
I said to him
with a broken heart.

His hands stretched out
    embraced me with love;
        "You are a better one than I,"
        said he to me.

Lesson from the Ants

Tens of thousands
    like an army they marched
Came from who knows where
    going where only they know.

An army of ants
climbing the wall
carrying their rice
and bits of food.

I sat down to watch
hoping to learn what I could.

No confusion
they marched well
to a tune they all knew.

They talked to each other
    with a touch of their bodies
    giving and receiving news
They seemed to show great love.

One ant fell and hurt himself
A whole group came to carry him
There were many of them
taking care of their wounded friend.

They could have said,
    "He is only one—
    let's forget him
    and finish our job."

Don't kill a wounded soldier,
    my friend
You too will someday be
    in his shoes.

Forgive

"Forgive him?
        No. Never.
        I cannot.
        I will not.
        How can I?"

Your words portray
        pain so deep
        through injustice you suffered
        from others' hands.

They robbed your rights
        slandered your name
        didn't keep their promises
        wounded you with words
            sharper than swords.
Your future is ruined
        your plans destroyed
        betrayed by those
            you trusted so much.

Memories are raw pain
    fresh each time
    an open wound
    your soul bleeds.

Sick in body
    mind and soul
Every cell
    defiled by bitterness.

Bitterness and hatred
    wishing for revenge
    eating you alive
    unbearable pain.

When you refuse to forgive
    those who wrong you,
    you let demons
        tear you apart.

How many have been hurt
    through your careless words
    things you did
    and things you didn't do?

continues

We are people
	with feet of clay
We all stand condemned
	before God's bright light.

Open your heart
	and hear Christ's words:
"Forgive others
as I have forgiven you."

Forgive, my friend,
	with all your heart
You will find peace
	and healing from Christ.

Sharp Words

I fold my hands
And beg of you
On bended knee
Have mercy on me.
Don't hurt me anymore
With words
So sharp
Sharper than a double-edged sword.

I ask of you now
To sit in my place
And feel my pain
Before you speak.
How can you be so numb
Not to care if I hurt?
If you were in my place
What would you wish?

continues

I cry all night long
All alone.
My children all died
My wealth is all gone.
My wife curses me
Innocent though I am.
My relatives failed me
Forsaken by friends.
My servants don't answer
I am skin and bones.

When will this all end?
Or be the end of me?
Until then,
Tell me a few words
Of hope and comfort
Please
I beg you on bended knees.

—Job 16, 19:2, Bible

When

When your heart is broken
When no one understands
When tears turn to rivers
When you lose all hope

There is someone who was broken
There is someone who understands
There is someone who cried
There is someone who is hope

His arms wide open
    with love and
        compassion
He calls you by name

To mend your broken heart
    And to wipe your tears
        And to give you hope.

Prayer of a Hurting Soul

You are the only one, O Lord
who sees and knows
the agony of my troubled heart
and You alone can make me whole.

I am tired and weary
exhausted and drained
for I don't know what to do
with problems I can't even define.

Your Word tells me You care
every hair on my heard is known to You.
Change my heart by Your grace
cause me to trust You no matter what.

Calm my troubled soul
with Your love and grace
heal my wounds by Your Word
Please help me feel I am safe.

Help me to cast away doubts and fears
and trust in Your love
that never changes
For You are sovereign and You keep Your Word.

Thank You for hearing the cry of my heart.
Your grace and love I receive now—
My heart is filled with faith, hope and love
I am so glad I am not alone.

Mask

He was not my friend
   but I wanted to help
   for he was sinking
   without hope.

He betrayed
   the friends he had
   played a double role
   now he was alone.

I reached out
   with all my heart
   to save the man
   I knew till then.

What I grabbed
   was a mask he wore
The mask came off
   he sank down into the depths
   he left me holding
   only his mask.

In the Long Run

If your faith is weak
    God will help
You will be strong
    in the long run.

If you are a fake
    insincere in heart
Even God cannot help
    in the long run.

ROSE
AND
THORNS

Why?

"Why?" is the question I most often asked
When bad things happened now and then.
Whatever way I could shift the blame
Was my way to find some peace.

A wayside salesman was selling his combs
"Come, buy my combs!" he called.
"What is so special about this one?" I asked.
"Why, it has the finest tooth you'll ever find."

The Word of God is the finest-toothed comb
With it, you can comb through your life.
Then "Why?" is a question you will never ask—
We all stand condemned in His bright light.

Don't Give Up

All is dark
    like a thousand nights
Gone too far
    there is no return
The bottom has dropped out
    the door slammed shut
Let me die.

If these are words
    that tell of your life,
Don't give up—
    there is hope for you.

God is not angry,
    He is on your side.
His Son has
    taken your place
To die
    that you may live.

Wind

It is summer again
    school is out
Kite-flying season
    is here again.

The wind is strong
    contrary it blows
That keeps the kite
    up in the sky.

It is the wind
    contrary to us
That helps us soar
    like eagles in the sky.

Seeds You Sow

A tiny seed
    in the ground below
I watched for weeks
    until it sprouted.

Inch by inch
    the tiny plant grew
Now leaves, now twigs
    for it was a teakwood tree.

Time moved on fast
    fifty years passed
Now a mighty tree
    under its shadow I sit.

A seed of habit you sow now
    no matter how tiny it is
Some day it will too
    cast a shadow on your life.

My Wardrobe

I opened the door
    to my wardrobe
    to get a shirt
    that matched my suit.

Among the expensive
    bright lovely clothes
    an old shirt peeked through
    that was faded and used.

Gray and old
    collar torn
    holes everywhere
    stitches out.

It has been there for
    twenty years
    hung unused for
    all these years.

I stood still
    with the closet open
    memories going back
    to the early seventies.

In North India
    with a few clothes
    living with a team
    working for God.

This was my best shirt
    during those years
    now it is old
    without any use.

I still keep it
    among the rest
    to remind me daily
    of those early years.

"Bless the LORD, O my soul,
and forget not all His benefits."

—Psalm 103:2, Bible

Same Source

There is no rose
    without the thorns.
The life of the rose
    and of the thorns
    are from the same source.

A bed of roses
    has destroyed as many lives
as did thorns
    of sorrow and pain.

So a saint prayed long ago:
    "Dear God,
    Please don't make me rich
        lest I forget you
    and don't make me poor
        that I go out and steal."

What Is Your Complaint?

You have eyes to read these words
Think of the blind who cannot see.

You have ears to hear the birds sing
Think of the deaf who cannot hear.

Legs to walk and run—you have them
Think about the ones with no legs at all.

Your mind is an absolute miracle
Think of the many who have lost their minds.

Your husband is not a loving man
Think of the women who don't have one.

Your children are a headache, you say
Think of those who don't have them.

Teacher, such troubles you tell me
Think of the unfortunate who can't go to school.

"This job is killing me," you say
Think of the millions who don't have a job.

continues

Your parents are mean and demanding
Think of those orphans on the Bombay streets.

You complain about your neighbors
Think of the lonely who live in the hills.

Your house is so small and crowded, you say
Think of the millions who live on the streets.

Buses and trains—what a headache—you are right!
But what would you prefer . . . to walk instead?

Thank You

Dear Jesus,
Thank You.

For the air we breathe,
The wonder of seeing and hearing
For big toes and small
    that help us stand up straight
For hands
    to write and touch,
The gifts of smell and taste.

Thank You

For clothes to wear
Food to eat
House to live in
Bed to sleep on
Pillow for my head
Sheet to cover me.

Clean water
Soap to clean myself
Toothpaste to brush with
Comb to run through my hair.

Thank You   *continues*

For friends I have
Parents who love
Neighbors
School and college
Teachers who guide.
Books to read
Buses and trains
Bicycles.

Wife
Husband
Children.

Church
And those who pray for me.

Oh, Lord, thank You
For angels guarding me
Safety on the road
Bad dreams that don't happen.

When I think of Your love
For me,
Your Son dying in my place
Forgiving my sins
saving my soul
Healing me

I thank You.

I LONG

TO **SEE**

YOU

Life in the City

Alarm clock
    time to get up
Motor bike
Car and gas
Time to go
Traffic light
Rush and run
Bus came late
Train is coming
    run you'll miss it
    it is late again

Children to school
    forgot their lunch
Who has the key?
Lock the door
Now all are gone
Parents are at work
Children at school
Dog in the cage
Cat in the house

Evening comes
    all return home
No time for nothing
Late to bed
Next day this way
    same as yesterday.

This is city life.
I am going back
    to my village I knew
to find my life

Face you know
name you know
they know you
    and smile at you

No phone to ring
small winding roads
flocks of birds
to sing all day

continues

Need some help
just shout it out
        a neighbor will come
for this is a village

For a short while
I went to the city
        to live there
        to know how life was

It is no life
        only a show
Nobody cares
        and you care for none

I think it is true
God intended for a man
        to live with nature
        to express real life.

Faithful Friend

The police came
and took him away.
His dog was sad
and followed after.

They put him in jail
for fourteen days.
The dog sat outside
crying for him.

Many tried their best
to call the dog away;
he wouldn't move
just sat there sad.

The man walked out
after serving his time;
His faithful friend
ran and jumped into his arms.

A true friend is one
Who will stay by you
When the sailing is rough
And in raging storms.

More Things Love Is . . .

Listening with your heart
Seeking to understand why
Forgiving
Long-suffering
Becoming the other person

Waiting
Overlooking faults
Silence
Being open and honest

Sharing in their need
Defending
Suffering when betrayed
Admitting faults and sin

Showing respect
Seeing the other side
Hoping through faith
Saying "no" and "you are wrong"

Valuing people for them, not what they do
Giving freedom to be themselves

Not intimidating
Being gentle
Soft words
Not jealous
Not arrogant
Not boastful
Being truthful and honest

Absence of fear
Restoring

Shavano

There was once a dog
Whose name was Shavano.
Loved by his mistress,
Who was a student.

Shavano would wait each day at the gate
Until she came home from her school.
The depth of love he expressed,
No one except his mistress knew.

Time went so fast
The student grew older
And so did her dog;
Yet they were closer than ever before.

Then one day, Shavano could no longer walk
The doctor said it was the end.
The news was told to the girl that day
She wept all night long.

The girl went to Shavano, early next morning.
She didn't say a word, but somehow he knew.
Tears fell from his blue eyes
The girl's tears fell on his furry neck.

It was time for school again
If she didn't go now the train would be gone.
She couldn't bear the thought of losing him forever;
Shavano mourned, with one last look.

Love anything, and your heart will break.
That is the price you must pay for love.
Not to love is not to live
And that is worse than a broken heart.

I love you no matter what the cost
Not blindly, because I know too much
I need your love more than you know
My heart may break—I am willing to risk it.

That girl was my wife when she was young
Shavano the dog was her loving friend
Shavano is no more, but the lesson is real
I too learned much from it all.

God loved the world that is lost in sin
His heart broke a million times
Yet He bore the pain alone
Because He is love and you He loved.

Missing You

Train, taxicab, reservations.
Plane ticket, suitcase, luggage tags.
Airport terminal.

Don't forget to call.
I love you too.
Whisper, hugs, tears.
Don't cry, I will call.

Immigration, final call.
Fasten seat belts, adjust your watch.
Temperature change.
Atlantic Ocean.
Runway, Autobahn.

Long-distance call
I can't wait to see you again.

Words that paint a thousand pictures
Reminding me once again that I am not home.
How lonely I feel
Nothing can take the place you fill.

It is true that we are pilgrims here;
Sometimes we all feel lonely and sad.
Although that is true, I must tell you—
Traveling alone is not pleasant at all.

My heart longs to see you again.
Home is where you are found.
I remember when Jesus said:
"Where a man's heart is, his treasure will also be."

And when it's all over and the journey ends,
I am so glad there is more to come.
No more good-byes or tears to wipe,
Finally we'll be together in that place—I am glad.

I Long to See You

Let Me Dream

I look for you
    everywhere I go
for I think of you
    more than you know.

Though you are not here
    you are here
as I close my eyes
    here with me now.

And in my dreams
    a thousand ways
wherever I go
    I have you with me.

I am with you
So let me dream.

My Father

The other day going through files
where old correspondence is kept,
There I saw a letter from my father
that he wrote before his death.

Memories of my father flooded my heart—
I am glad he was my dad.
He was strong, yet so kind
A man of integrity—known to all.

I can't remember him ever saying words
such as, "I love you, son,"
But I knew he loved me from his look
and with words he didn't say.

It has been nearly four decades
since he passed away
and how I wish
he was with us now.

More Little Things I Like

Children waving from school buses
Smiling at strangers
    and seeing them smile back

Watching ants and the way they live
Squirrels running up the tree and
    making noise

Handwriting I can read
A dog wagging its tail
A firm handshake

Hearing someone say,
    "Thank you"
    "I am sorry"
    "That is a secret—I can't tell you," and
    "Please"

Singing in the shower
A good joke
A queue that moves fast

Eating peanuts
Riding a bike
Cold coffee in summer
Bathing in the rain

Running into an old friend from school
Listening to people

A clean toilet
Tiny flashlight
Folk songs
Smelling a rose
Killing flies

Walking in snow
A neat home
Asking many "Why" questions

Listening to children
Sleeping when I'm tired
Soft water
Hot soup in winter

Thinking about the one I
Forgiving my enemies
Feeling that peace

Because

Because I care
    I think of you
Because I think
    I pray for you
Because I pray
    I long to see you
    and all
    that God is doing through you.

Don't Forget

Don't forget
the words of kindness
others have spoken to you;

Don't forget
those in need of kindness;
speak kindly to them.

Don't forget
the many who helped you
in your time of need;

Don't forget
to help the one
who is in need that you know.

Don't forget
the prayers of concern
someone offered for you;

Don't forget
to pray for those
you know who are in need.

continues

Don't forget—
life is short,
it will soon be gone;

Don't forget
to live for Christ
as this may be
        the last day
you have.

TIME WAITS

FOR

NO ONE

Final Words

So many came
to say their last good-byes
    for he had friends
    from all walks of life.

I stood with the rest
by the grave
    the casket was lowered
    and wailing broke out.

A preacher in a black suit
talked to the man
    in the casket
    who couldn't hear:

"You who were made
out of the dust
    return to the dust
    until the last day."

Silence.
Sounds of mourning
    the crowd slowly dispersed
    each one lost in his own sorrow.

I was alone
going back home
        asked a few questions
        to my own mind:

"What happened
        to the deed to his house
        to the keys to his car
        to his wallet with money
        to his deposits in the bank
        to his shares and bonds
        to the checkbook with his name
        to the pen that he owned?"

Naked he came
Alone he came
        into this world
        alone did he return . . .

        and so will you.

Stranger in My Own World

Stranger in my own world I am
Like a child lost in the crowd
Lost in the desert
Lost in nothing
Lightning strike deep in my heart
I am so afraid.

Stranger in my own land I am
Like the prodigal all alone
Friends I thought were there
But now I know it was not so
And I am left alone all is lost
I am so afraid.

Stranger in my own lotus
Of dreams and hopes
I thought would satisfy
Sun went down
Petals closed up
Is there a way out?
I am so afraid.

Stranger in my own world no more
For you, my Lord—came in
Afraid I was to open the door
But Your love made it open
Darkness fled
I am free
Found life in love
Full of grace
I am no more alone.

I Could Have . . .

I planted an oak
    twenty years ago
Now it is grown
    to a full tree.

I could have planted one
    thirty years ago
Not just one
    but a dozen or more.

Time waits for no one
    no matter who he is
Do what could be done
    the time is now.

Tomorrow

"Tomorrow I will do it,"
    he said to me
     and tomorrow came
but he died yesterday.

This Old Watch

I have a watch that is fifty years old
The man who first owned it died long ago
To have a watch was unusual then
Only the rich could afford such things.

They say he cared for it like his life
He wouldn't give it to anyone, even to see,
Fearing they might wind it or let it fall
His children complained that he loved it too much.

One day it stopped and he was depressed
He went to a shop to get it repaired.
"It will be ready for you in a week," he was told
He could not leave it, for he loved it so.

He went to another place and stayed all day
Watching his watch being taken apart
He refused to leave until it was fixed like new
Now he was happy, with his dear watch.

One day at ten o'clock he had a stroke
They took him to the hospital with lightning speed
Minutes passed as hours and days
He did not look at his watch anymore.

The doctor said he did the best he could
But the man was dead within a few hours' time
And as they sang the last farewell song
Someone removed his watch from his wrist.

That watch outlived the one had owned it
Palaces remain while kings come and go
Man is the most fragile thing I know
Once he is broken, no one can fix him.

Too Late

With my dad
I went to fish
I was young
Barely five.

Often we went
Late in the night
He threw the net
I shone the light.

Of all the times
That we would go
I can't remember
A word he said.

I wish he had spoken
As father to son
Now he is dead
And I am sad.

I wish I knew him
But it is too late.

Dance Not for Time

Up in the tree
　　the leaves were green
　　full of life
　　dancing in the wind.

A tiny bird came
　　and sat on a leaf
The leaf broke off
The bird flew away.

Life is so fragile
　　like a tiny leaf
One little germ
　　one small ache
　　one fall
can end your life.

Present is passing
Nothing is forever
　　Dance not for time
　　But for Eternity.

Raining Again

It is monsoon again
>I sit alone on my bed
>looking through the window
>watching the downpour.

It is late afternoon
>the sky is angry and dark
>the wind is blowing strong
>a tree branch has fallen.

Lightning shoots through the sky
>thunder roars
>the earth shakes
>I am scared.

My mind travels back in time
>thinking of my childhood
>when I was a young boy
>going to school.

Nonstop rain
>my umbrella was old
>had some holes in it
>made me wet.

Crossing the ferry
    walking all the way
    reached my school
    with a friend.

All that happened
    a long time ago.
Now it is monsoon again.

Memories of my past
    make me wish
I was little again.

The End of the Race

He says,

> "I am ready to go,
> No regrets, none.
> This race was long
> the battle was tough
> But I didn't give up
> nor did I look back.

> "I kept my focus
> I paid the price
> blood, sweat and agony.
> Yes, it was worth it all.

> "I see Him waiting for me
> with my reward in
> His nail-pierced hand."

BE **STILL**

AND KNOW THAT

I AM

GOD

Surrender

"No longer will I
yield to you,"
said Moon
to Sun.

"No longer do I want
to be used by you
to shine your light.
I am not your slave."

Night came.
Earth looked for Moon,
but she hid herself—
and it was dark.

The sky was black
Earth was sad.
Moonless sky—
None looked up.

Moon was Moon
because of Sun.
She didn't want to yield
and became a black hole.

It is only in surrender
to Christ the Son
that you will find
meaning in life.

Stubborn Fish

I chew the fish down
    to my stomach below
    my gastric juices were ready
to dissolve it for good.

The fish told the juices
    to get out of the way
    for he didn't want to become
part of me.

They argued and fought
    for a long time
    the fish was stubborn
and would not yield.

Finally the gastric juices gave it up
    and told the headquarters to do the rest
    within few minutes noises started
and I threw up the stubborn fish.

Now he ended up unused and wasted
    sent down the toilet
    with a blast of fresh water
never to be seen again.

Had the fish yielded
    to the juices to dissolve him down
    he could have become part of me
to write this poem
that you may well need.

To save yourself
    is to lose your life.
Give it away for others for Christ's sake
    and you shall find life.

Peace

Life is peaceful
when you know
there is nothing
between you and God.

Life is washed
in the blood of Christ
cleansing every sin
making you whole.

Who I Am

What I am
What I am not
Things I have
Things I have not
My gifts
My limitations
My strengths
My weaknesses

I accept
    humbly now
who I am
    in God's plan.
No more
    no less
Content I am
    in His love.

Sparrow

That evening

I was playing
with my children
in front of our house
in our yard
under the tree.
Sparrows were chirping—
we looked up
and saw their nest
up in the tree.
There she sat,
motionless,
two tiny birds
under her wings.

That night

> no star in the sky—
> darkness reigned
> from its throne.
> A storm roared through
> trees shook
> branches fell.
> The sky grew angry
> clapped its hands
> lightning shot out
> thunder growled.
> Clouds burst open
> and began to weep
> in a great downpour—
> no letting up.

continues

Next morning

The rain had stopped
the sun rose.
I went out
to look for the birds.
Soaking wet
she sat in the nest
two tiny heads
peeking through her wing.
Was she sleeping?
"Oh, no," I thought.
"She can't be dead, can she?"

Yes, she died in the rain.
She could have escaped, but
for the love of her children,
she gathered them under her wings
to save their lives.

The love of the sparrow
touched my heart.
How much greater
is the love of God!
Christ died
in our place
that we might live.

Slavery

Wanting things
　　you don't have
Buying things
　　you don't need
With money
　　you don't have
To impress others
　　who don't care

Is to become a slave
　　of greed and pride
Is vanity of vanities
　　in a passing world.

"But rather seek ye
the kingdom of God;
and all these things
　　shall be added unto you. . . .

For where your treasure is,
there will your heart be also."

　　　　—Jesus (Luke 12:31, 34, Bible)

His Grace

In the hollow of a tree
was a nest hidden away,
made by two birds
to lay their eggs.

A cozy home
for their young;
with dreams and hopes
they built it with love.

A snake discovered the tree
and the nest in the hollow;
he slithered his way up
to eat the young ones.

Miles up in the sky
a hawk circled and soared;
with piercing eyes
he watched the snake's movement.

As the snake inched his way
into the hollow,
the hawk swooped down,
snatched the snake away
with his powerful claws.

God cared for the tiny birds;
His angel sent the hawk to rescue
them.

God cares for you;
trust in His grace.

Things That Make Me Happy

Watching bats
    sucking nectar from banana flowers
    in the evening
Watching nonstop rain
    from my poomugam*
Plucking fruit from trees
    near my home
Talking to poor people
    who need help

Kneeling in worship
    when I pray
Meeting an old man or woman
    who really knows God
Seeing the old coconut trees
    I used to climb on
    when I was five or six

Driving my 1962 Volkswagen Bug
    with the windows open
Riding my bicycle
    around the seminary
Relaxing in my study
    and listening to folk music

Spending time with people
>who are truly humble

Meeting old friends I served with
>on mission teams in the late sixties
>and recalling our old stories

The atmosphere of holy awe
>during Holy Communion
>and feeling that I am sitting with Christ
>in the Upper Room

Seeing my leaders do better than me
>makes me feel at peace for the future

Taking time to be silent for hours
>sitting down in my poomugam to think deeply

Looking up at night
>and seeing millions of bright stars
>sparkle all across the sky and think
>beyond time!

Traditions, signs and symbols
>that make me part of the Ancient Church

*A *poomugam* is a special type of front porch common to many
very old houses in the South Indian village where I grew up.

Carried

I saw the cat carrying its kittens
    ever so gently
        from place to place.

I saw the sparrow sitting in her nest
    over her little ones
        in spite of the rain.

I saw the hen gathering her chicks
    under her wings
        at the sighting of the crow.

I saw the monkey leaping from branch to branch
    holding her baby
        so it won't fall.

I saw myself
    so helpless
        and fragile
Held so tightly by an unseen hand.

I looked up into His face—
Jesus, full of love and grace.

Be Still and Know

A thousand voices screaming at me
    to meet their demands
    to move faster than I was able
I became a restless soul.

A thousand times I was tempted
    to throw up my hands
    to give up all hope
to lay down and die.

A thousand nights of silence
    engulfed my soul
    forced me to kneel
to pray beside my bed.

A thought like sun's brightness
    flooded my soul
    He spoke gently in my ear,
    "Be still and know I am God."

Silence

I heard silence speaking to me
    to be silent
    to question my soul
    to hear the voice of God.

It is late after midnight
I've been sitting alone
leaning against the wooden pillars
in my poomugam* in utter silence.

In silence His voice I heard
    of love and mercy
    correction and comforts.
Peace filled my soul.

*see page 235

O GOD,
HOW
GREAT
YOU ARE

A Simple Question

It was by a dry well that I saw the young lad.
I asked for his name, he told me what it was.
"How old are you?" I asked.
"Nine and a half," he said.

His baby face told me how innocent he was.
I enjoyed his bouncy spirit as he talked with me.
"What do you do?" He replied, "I go to school."
"Why school?" I asked. "To learn," he replied.

And now I posed even more questions to him:
"Why do you want to learn; can you tell me?"
"Of course I can," he said. "So I can be smart."
"Why do you want to be smart?"
    He said, "To get a good job."

"Good job?" I probed—his reply was fast:
"So I can earn lots of money in a short time."
"Why do you want money?" I shot back at him.
His answer was quick—"To buy food."

Before I could think, he spoke my mind:
"You will ask, 'Why food,' right?
The answer is simple," he said. "So I can eat."
He laughed, saying he had thought quicker than I.

continues

Now the next question was coming, he knew.
And he was ready with an answer again.
"Why do I eat?" he said boldly.
"So like you and others, I too can live."

"My dear boy," I replied, "how smart you are.
I truly admire your courage.
Now, I will ask only one more question.
Answer me this one and I will leave you alone."

He nodded his head with pride and confidence.
I simply asked, "And why do you live?"
After my question, he didn't answer back,
Looking down began searching his mind.

Deep in thought he remained for a time;
After a while, with all sereneness,
He looked straight into my eyes

And simply said,
"Sir, why do I live? To die."

What would you answer if I were to ask you,
"My good friend, why do you live?"
If you know Jesus, then you surely can say,
for me to live is Christ and die is gain.

The Earth Is Filled with Your Love

—Psalm 119:64, Bible

> Music of the mountain
> Colors of the rainbow
> The sound of waterfalls
> The songs of birds
> Look of a loving dog
> Dark green grass
> Loving eyes
> Gentle touch
> Caring words
> Soft answer
> Soothing music
> Poems that touch the heart
> Gentle breeze on my face
> Someone who truly loves
> Someone to love deeply
> Innocence of a child

continues

Unselfish acts
Unexpected gifts
Surprise that makes me glad
Hope realized
Dreams of hope
Beautiful flowers
Blue sky
Starry night
Feelings of happiness
Happy faces with smiles
Loving embrace
Hearing, "I love you too"
Answered prayers
Unanswered prayers
Trials that help me grow
Clear seeing
Seasons in life

The Cross

Creator became creation
Holiness became sin
Innocent pronounced guilty
Life-giver killed by sin and hate

Trinity was broken
Father forsakes His Son
His friends ran away
Left all alone to suffer

Bloody and wounded
His back plowed over
Flesh from His body torn
Blood pouring out

continues

Fairest among 10,000
Disfigured from abuse
Human, He no more looked
My Savior and Lord

The cross was heavy
Fell He along the way
He chose Calvary
To redeem me from sin

I stood by the cross
Looked into His bloody face
He looked at me
With love so tender full of grace

I understood then
He took my place
To make me His
I am no more my own . . .

Loved by You

To be loved by You
To be in love with You
To live in Your love
It is by far the most joyous thing I know.

"Follow Me," my ears heard
Your voice of love and care,
"Take My hand." I respond:
"I will follow You all the way."

For so long tried I to find
Answer to life and pain
To understand meanings
To find a reason to live.

Having You beside me
Gives me strength to live,
For Your love fills my life
Surrounds me with peace.

Overwhelmed by Your love
My world a better place
Sunshine breaking forth
Can't hide my joy anymore.

Alone

Standing alone
on the deck of the ship
looking into the sky
full of stars.

The ocean was calm
a gentle breeze came
touching my face
in the silence of night.

Quiet rippling waves
talking to me
with words only they knew
but touching me with peace.

What majesty
the beauty of it all
causes me to say,
"O God, how great You are."

If this book has been a blessing,
I would really like to hear from you.
Please send me an email at kp@gfa.org.

Index

Other Books by K.P. Yohannan

Revolution in World Missions

Step into the story of missionary statesman K.P. Yohannan and experience the world through his eyes. You will hang on every word—from the villages of India to the shores of Europe and North America. Watch out: His passion is contagious!

No Longer a Slumdog

Meet an abandoned girl who found hope at the end of the railroad tracks, a young boy who escaped after years of forced servitude and others whose lives have been redeemed. You'll be captivated by this powerful move of God as K.P. Yohannan leads you through the slums and villages of South Asia into the hearts and lives of these precious children.

Living in the Light of Eternity

This book will challenge you to look beyond temporary concerns of life to what will last forever. You will gain a solid basis for genuine spiritual growth as you learn to organize your priorities in the light of eternity.

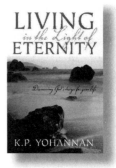

The Road to Reality

For more than two decades, *The Road to Reality* has helped thousands to escape from the "plastic Christianity" of our age. This prophetic and practical book will point you to the road back to authentic New Testament Christianity and help you take your first steps toward living with simplicity and purpose.

Touching Godliness

If you yearn for genuine godliness in your life, this book is a must-read! Writing with fatherly concern, K.P. Yohannan challenges us to follow Christ down the path of total surrender and submission and, in the end, find God's promised "life abundant."

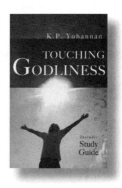

Reflecting His Image

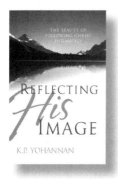

Does it feel like life is closing in on you? K.P. Yohannan shows you the way to rise above the weight of this world and keep your true purpose in clear view. Relevant and incredibly practical, the short easy-to-read chapters make this book an ideal daily devotional.

Order these and other titles online at www.gfa.org/B10

If you were touched by this book and want to hear more from the author, be sure to visit our resource page for free downloads.

Free messages

Ebooks

Videos

MP3s

... and more by K.P. Yohannan to help you go deeper in your spiritual life.

Venture into new territory in your walk with Christ!

www.gfa.org/resource